NATIONAL GEOGRAPHIC

Ladders

SUPER
STRUCTURES

Wonders

The Great Pyramid is in Giza, Egypt. The base of the Great Pyramid would cover seven city blocks today.

Machu Picchu is in the mountains of Peru. Most of its building stones were heavy granite. They are extremely hard to cut, even with today's technology.

by Barbara Keeler

Imagine building a tall wall, snakelike across the United States from New York City to Seattle. Or think about moving huge stone blocks the size of small rooms. Now imagine doing these things without modern machines! People long ago figured out how.

Angkor Wat is a temple in the forests of Cambodia. Its likeness appears on the nation's flag today.

The Great Wall of China spans the entire country. Work on the Great Wall began about 600 B.C. Work did not stop until 1600 A.D.

Without the tools or technology builders use today, ancient people built giant, well-engineered structures of breathtaking beauty. Many still stand. How did they do it? Why did they do it? Let's explore just four of what might be called "wonders of the ancient world."

THE GREAT PYRAMID

Picture a group of ancient workers at the bottom of the Great Pyramid, the largest of these three in the picture. With a square base and triangular sides, this pyramid stands almost as high as a 50-story building. Workers crane their necks to see the top. They plan to haul a huge block of stone, called a capstone, to the peak. The **mass** of the stone is about 2.3 metric tons (2.5 tons), about the same as a medium-sized truck today.

The pyramid's walls were built from limestone, which was easier than other kinds of rock to cut, carve, and polish. Workers used metal chisels to cut limestone blocks. The pointed capstone was made of a very hard rock, such as granite. To cut granite, workers used another hard rock—dolerite—to chip slots around the shape of the granite they wanted. Workers shoved wooden pegs into the slots and filled them with water. The pegs swelled and cracked the granite. Then new slots could be made and the process repeated.

A polished limestone covering gave pyramids a shiny appearance. Covering stones were removed about 600 years ago. Egyptians used them to build new structures.

4

The limestone and granite blocks had to be moved from the mines to the building site. The limestone mine was only about 20 kilometers (12 miles) away. The granite came from mines about 900 kilometers (560 miles) away! Granite blocks were loaded onto boats and floated down the Nile River. Workers used tracks and ropes to move all of the blocks to the building site. Then with ropes and ramps, workers hauled the blocks up the sides of the pyramid.

Why build such a huge structure? For a tomb. As soon as a pharaoh, or Egyptian ruler, came to power, he started building his tomb! King Khufu's Great Pyramid took nearly 20 years to complete. A pyramid contained the mummified body of the pharaoh and, according to ancient Egyptian beliefs, materials to sustain his spirit in the afterlife.

147 m (480 ft.)

- Workers hauled more than 2 million stone blocks.
- Some blocks weighed as much as 45 metric tons (50 tons).
- When new, the Great Pyramid of King Khufu stood 147 meters (480 feet) tall.

Great Wall of China

If the various sections of the Great Wall of China were stretched out straight, its 21,000 kilometers (13,000 miles) would reach about halfway around the world! For over 2,000 years, Chinese emperors directed the building of the wall to protect China from northern invaders.

The entire wall was not built from scratch, however. Parts of it connected existing fortresses and natural barriers. Builders used local materials, so different sections were built of soil, stone, or brick. When they could, builders used stone, because stone could better hold weight and fend off attacks.

- The Great Wall, shown in green, is made up of many sections.
- Trenches, rivers, and steep hills make up parts of the wall.
- The wall protected China's culture from outside influence.

The part of the wall in the photograph is more than long; it is tall and thick. It is between 5 and 9 meters (15 and 30 feet) tall and between 5 and 8 meters (15 and 25 feet) wide. Towers rise above it at regular intervals. They were used as watchtowers and signal towers. Archers defended the wall, and sentries along the walls warned against coming invasions. Fortresses were built along the route. A 4-meter- (13-foot-) wide roadway runs along the top of some sections. That is wide enough for five horses to walk side by side. Troops and messengers could travel quickly along this smooth path in the rugged countryside.

One watchtower is placed about every kilometer (one-half mile) in this section of the wall.

- Machu Picchu was built during the early 1400s.
- Around 750–1,000 people could have lived in the city.
- When first built, the city would have gleamed white in the green jungle.

Terraces, or stair-step designs, kept soil from washing away.

MACHU PICCHU

Some wonders of the world still leave experts wondering. Machu Picchu is one of them. Why was it built? How was it used? Historians are not sure. The Inca had no written language, so they left no records. Experts are not even sure how ancient builders managed to construct the complex with no iron, steel, or wheels. About 140 buildings—mostly houses, but also some temples—blend into the mountainscape.

The city stands on a granite plateau about 2,500 meters (8,000 feet) above sea level in the Peruvian Andes. From there, the Inca could observe events below in the Urubamba Valley. They could also spot enemy forces in the valley without being seen. From below, the city was hidden from view.

The Inca took advantage of the white granite of the mountain. They made small white granite bricks and put them together without any mortar, or material to stick them together. The bricks are so well-fitted that often a knife blade cannot fit between them. The builders probably made holes in the rocks and inserted wet wooden wedges. Next, they waited for the water to freeze. Because the ice had greater **volume** than water, it forced the rock slabs apart. Then the builders had to make the bricks smooth and straight enough to fit together well.

Builders also engineered walls, terraces, and ramps. These structures preserved soil, conserved water, and helped people grow crops. Some original irrigation systems still work today.

Angkor Wat

Deep in the lush forests of Cambodia's Siem Reap province, the huge, sprawling city of Angkor once thrived from the ninth to the fifteenth centuries. Evidence from aerial photographs and radar show that Angkor once covered about 1,000 square kilometers (400 square miles). That would make it almost as big as the city of Los Angeles in the United States.

What, then, is a wat? *Wat* is a Khmer word for "temple" or "school." The massive Angkor Wat is not only the most famous of Angkor's 74 temples. It's the most famous of all of Cambodia's temples. It was built between 1113 and 1150 A.D. to honor the Hindu god Vishnu.

This photograph shows just a portion of the temple.

- Angkor had an enormous system of artificial canals, dikes, and reservoirs.
- The temple was guarded by a 6.4-kilometer (4-mile) moat.
- The water system provided water to grow rice—Angkor's money.

Builders used blocks of local materials for the temple and other stone structures. Many blocks were carved from soft sandstone in the area. Unfortunately, many of the sandstone blocks have crumbled in the hundreds of rainy seasons since they were made. But the land offered other materials, too. Builders cut laterite—a wet, spongy layer of soil—into blocks using a spade. The blocks dried into hard stones that could be fitted together without mortar. They weren't as affected by the rainy seasons. The surrounding forests provided wood to build structures that weren't sacred. Builders placed wooden neighborhood homes on mounds to protect them from flooding.

←————————————| Originally, Angkor Wat's towers would have been covered in gold.

Check In How did builders take advantage of the local area to construct these wonders?

How Tall!

by Jennifer K. Cocson

A city with little vacant land has nowhere to grow but up. Cities are indeed growing up, with skyscrapers soaring ever higher. Over the last 100 years, engineers have been solving problem after problem to build taller and taller.

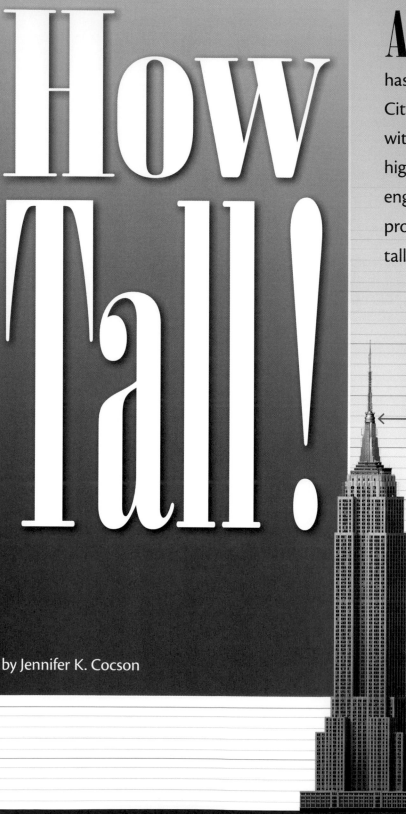

442 m
(1,451 ft.)

381 m
(1,250 ft.)

EMPIRE STATE BUILDING

New York City,
United States

WILLIS TOWER

Chicago,
United States

What problems? Weight, windows, and wind. The invention of materials with **properties** such as strength and flexibility allows engineers to design in new and different ways. The designs distribute the weight of the materials in such ways that allow big windows. As skyscrapers grow taller, wind pushes on them harder. Today's tallest skyscrapers must be 50 times stronger against wind than a 20-story building 60 meters (200 feet) tall.

Height poses another problem—how to get to the top. The solution? Elevators, of course!

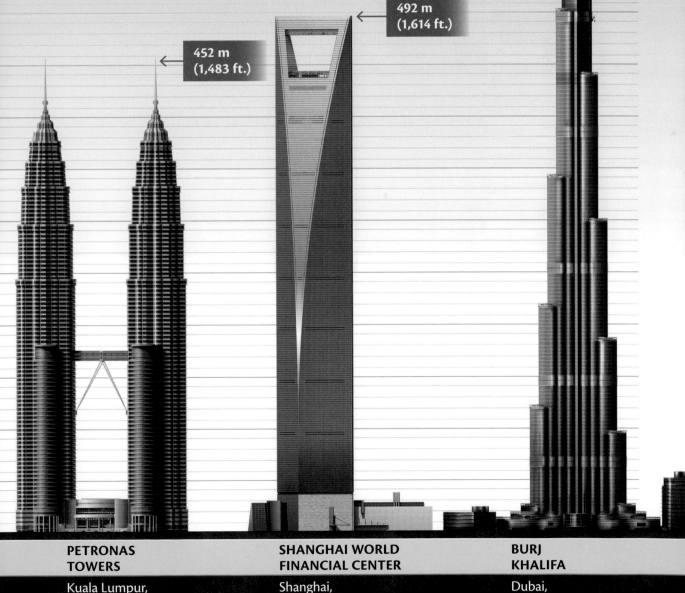

828 m
(2,717 ft.)

492 m
(1,614 ft.)

452 m
(1,483 ft.)

PETRONAS TOWERS

Kuala Lumpur, Malaysia

SHANGHAI WORLD FINANCIAL CENTER

Shanghai, China

BURJ KHALIFA

Dubai, United Arab Emirates

Petronas Towers

About 33,500 metric tons (36,900 tons) of steel support the concrete columns of the buildings' skeleton. That amount of steel is more than what 3,000 elephants weigh!

3,000

Think of making a square out of eight school buses. That's how big the high-strength concrete column is in the center of each building.

No, you are not seeing double! These buildings, the Petronas Towers, are the world's tallest twin towers. Each tower has 88 stories and a tall spire. Double-decker elevators let people off at odd and even floors at the same time.

A skybridge links the two towers. More than 40 stories up, the skybridge is higher than the top of the Great Pyramid! You might think dangerous wind storms would damage the bridge, but engineers thought of that. They designed the bridge so that it can slide inside one of the towers during heavy wind.

Be glad you do not have to wash the windows! Between them, the towers have 32,000 windows. Washing each tower just once takes window washers a whole month. Stainless steel sun shades help block some of the bright sunlight.

Shanghai
World Financial Center

The opening at the top of the building solves a problem! The opening allows the wind to blow through the building rather than pushing on it. The top of the opening forms the floor of the highest observation deck in the world! Its walls slant outward so you feel like you could fall out—but no way.

The building offers more than 372,000 square meters (4,000,000 square feet) of space for stores and offices. That would cover more than 27 football fields.

The Shanghai World Financial Center started out as a mere 94-story building. Then a lull in construction halted work.

When construction started back up, builders wanted to top another skyscraper that was being built. But the foundation's design could support only so much weight. Height was capped at 101 stories.

Over 10,000 windows withstand earthquakes, typhoon-strength winds, extreme weather, and the sun's rays. A specially-developed glue-type sealer attaches the windows to the aluminum frame.

The building looks like a giant bottle opener—and guess what? You can buy bottle openers in the shape of the building!

The building is also designed to hold up in an earthquake. It resembles a giant square column near the bottom. Starting about one-third of the way up, the sides gradually taper closer together until they nearly meet and form a narrow rectangle at the top.

Burj Khalifa

Unlike other super skyscrapers, Burj Khalifa includes residential space. Does it surprise you that it has less floor space than the Shanghai World Financial Center, which is 59 stories shorter? This is partly because Burj Khalifa narrows as it gets taller. The shape and the narrowing make it harder for the wind to push against the building. It was also turned slightly compared to the original plans to lessen the effect of the winds.

Soaring more than 805 meters (one-half mile) into the sky, Burj Khalifa (Khalifa Tower) is about twice as high as the Empire State Building! Burj Khalifa has 163 stories above the ground and a tall spire that can be seen from 95 kilometers (60 miles) away. Its observation deck is sky-high, too, and visitors can look down on ant-sized people scurrying along the sidewalk.

Rainwater is recycled. Water vapor in the air conditioning system condenses, or turns to liquid. Then it is collected and used to water the grounds. The water collected each year could fill 20 Olympic-sized swimming pools.

The outside is covered with a reflective glaze of aluminum and stainless steel to lessen the effect of extreme summer temperatures.

Burj Khalifa has 57 elevators, one with the longest travel distance in the world.

57

Check In Compare the ways that Petronas Towers, Shanghai World Financial Center, and Burj Khalifa are designed to prevent wind damage.

HOW Small!

by Judy Elgin Jensen

Around the world, many people live in houses that cover an area of about 11 square meters (120 square feet). That's less than half the size of a large school bus. While many reasons influence the size of people's homes, more and more are choosing to "live small." Why? The environment has a lot to do with it. Smaller homes require less space. They also require fewer **resources** to build them. And they cost less to heat, cool, clean, and maintain.

This front door leads to a large room covered by a loft. It's small size means you might not even need a permit to build it.

Inspired by the structure of a billboard, these tiny homes can be located anywhere. As Earth's population grows, people might build them in unusual places. Or perhaps they might build up above someone else's back yard!

Tree-house living in this private park allows others to continue to enjoy the grounds. Large windows allow the winter sun to warm the living space. In summer, the leafy trees keep the inside shaded—and cooler.

Many small homes are prefabricated, or built somewhere else and brought to the site almost complete. Prefabricating homes in a factory allows resources to be shared among several homes. Construction is often quicker, too. Trucking this finished house to its coastal location causes less damage to the beach than building it here.

Check In How might a tiny home be a good choice for the environment?

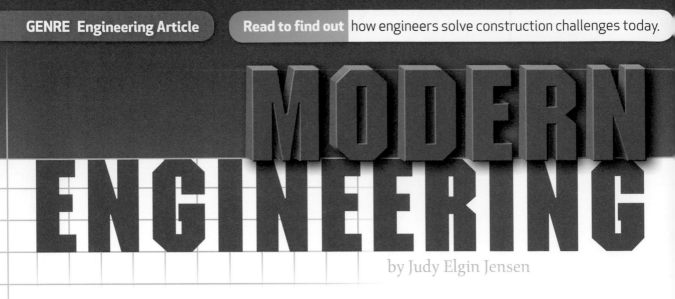

MODERN ENGINEERING

by Judy Elgin Jensen

Fast forward a few thousand years from the building of the Great Pyramid. It's the late 1800s, and the big problem of the day is how to move goods quickly from New York City to San Francisco without going all the way around the tip of South America. The longer goods took to reach their selling point, the more people had to pay for them. Sailing around the tip of South America was dangerous, too. How to cut the time? Find a shorter route.

BUILDING THE PANAMA CANAL

Engineers designed the Panama Canal to cut across the **isthmus,** or narrowest part, of Panama. Laboring in a steamy jungle, workers used rock drills, dynamite, and steam shovels to dig it.

FEATS

Soil and rock were unstable and sometimes slid down the hillsides. Heavy rains and runoff caused a river along the path of the canal to flood. To solve this problem, builders created a huge dam across the river. The dam created a huge artificial lake and controlled much of the river's flooding.

By 1914, the first ship sailed through the canal—the first of many that boosted the trade of countries around the world. Ships cut a two-week passage around South America to about ten hours. Ships traveled through a series of locks, or sets of gates that open and close to let boats in. Inside the locks, water levels can be raised or lowered to raise or lower a ship.

Engineers and builders in 1904 had technologies such as heavy machinery.

PANAMA CANAL EXPANSION

The Panama Canal was so successful it eventually could not keep up with the traffic. By the 2000s, about 14,000 ships were carrying ocean cargo through the Panama Canal each year. Unfortunately, the canal was not built to handle so much traffic. At both entrances, traffic jams slowed the world's ocean trade. Some ships waited as long as a week to enter the clogged canal. The cost was huge—as much as $40,000 a day to operate some of these ships. Another problem was that the locks were too small. In 1914, the largest ships fit into the locks like an ice cube in its tray. Later, global shippers built larger vessels that could not fit into the locks.

The canal is too small to accommodate modern cargo ships. This expansion will solve the problem.

In October 2006, Panama's citizens voted to expand the canal with completion targeted for 2014—100 years after its original opening. The canal will have larger locks, two new channels, and deeper, wider shipping lanes. Despite annual rainfall of about 254 centimeters (100 inches), the biggest challenge for engineers is saving water. The area around the canal supplies drinking water to 95 percent of the nearby population. Filling the locks uses more than 7.6 billion liters (2 billion gallons) of water per day, and bigger locks could double that. Therefore, engineers designed a system to capture and reuse 60 percent of the water as the locks are emptied.

Allowing bigger boats and more traffic through the canal will boost trade worldwide. The tolls for the canal will provide a rich source of income for Panama.

FRANCE'S MILLAU VIADUCT

On the Millau Viaduct, the world's tallest bridge, cars whiz along almost 250 meters (820 feet) above the floor of the Tarn Valley in France. Sometimes rising above the clouds, the tall towers support cables that hold up the bridge. The highest point on the bridge is taller than the Eiffel Tower!

The bridge solved a big problem for tourists, freight carriers, and other drivers traveling between Paris, France, and Barcelona, Spain. Without the bridge, drivers had to pick their way along twisty roads. The roads ran down and through the deep valley. Traffic often jammed and slowed drivers to a crawl. The area had become a bottleneck. Today, the bridge cuts the time to travel and transport goods through southern France by as much as four hours.

Of four possible routes crossing the Tarn Valley, votes were cast for the "high road" and work began. Support piers grew 4 meters (12 feet) every three days. Then roadway deck sections moved from east *and* west on special sliders at 9 meters (30 feet) per hour during nonstop 48-hour sessions. Stretched steel cables made up of seven twisted steel strands each anchor the deck. A wax-and-plastic coating protects the cables against rust. Weather strips stop water from trickling down the cables, which could cause dangerous vibrations in the bridge during high winds.

Most of the 2,460 meters (8,070 feet) of roadway deck was built at ground level. This was safer for workers.

VENICE UNDER WATER

Imagine a city without roads or cars! The city of Venice sprawls over a group of islands in the Lagoon of Venice in Italy. The lagoon stretches between the Adriatic Sea and several rivers. A strip of land shelters the city from the rough waters of the Adriatic. Even so, enough tidal water surges in and out to provide a natural sewerage system. Tides flush out the city's canals twice a day.

Without cars or roads, how would you get around a city of small islands? Venetians use canals and bridges. Instead of cars, they ride in boats.

Venice has long been and still is a seaport and home to a fishing industry. Historically, the city was also a great center of art, architecture, and Italian culture. Its present economy depends heavily on tourists. Tourists flock to see its canals, its ancient art treasures, and its ancient architecture.

THE PROBLEM

The sea, so important to the economy, culture, and history of the city, has also become a threat. The land has been sinking to lower levels and the waters of the Adriatic Sea have been rising. Sidewalks, homes, businesses, palaces, and churches have been flooded several times a year. Irreplaceable art and architecture are at risk from the floods. So are homes and businesses. So is the economy.

VENICE'S PROJECT MOSE

THE SOLUTION "With this scheme, we will save Venice," said one engineer. "It's the first time that this has been tried. The whole world is watching." She was referring to Project MOSE. Italian leaders hope Project MOSE can save art, architecture, homes, and the economy.

In 2003, engineers began designing 78 giant hollow steel gates on hinges. They would be placed across three inlets through which Adriatic tidewater surges into the lagoon. When raised before high tides, they would prevent the tides from flooding the city.

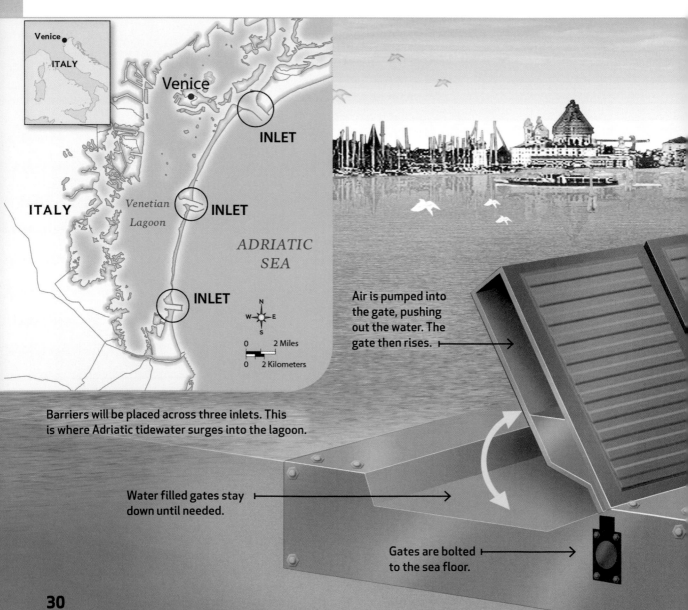

Barriers will be placed across three inlets. This is where Adriatic tidewater surges into the lagoon.

Air is pumped into the gate, pushing out the water. The gate then rises.

Water filled gates stay down until needed.

Gates are bolted to the sea floor.

Solutions often create additional problems, and some experts fear Project MOSE might threaten the health of people and fish. Raising the gates, they predict, will prevent the tides from flushing out the canals, creating a sewage problem. The nutrients sewage contains feed organisms that use up the oxygen. Supporters, however, say raising the gates temporarily will cause very little pollution and oxygen loss. They predict that the tides will quickly restore the lagoon and canals after the gates are lowered.

The results of engineering solutions are not fully known until they are tried. Engineers know that solutions such as the Panama Canal have solved transportation problems. They hope that Project MOSE will solve the problem of flooding in Venice.

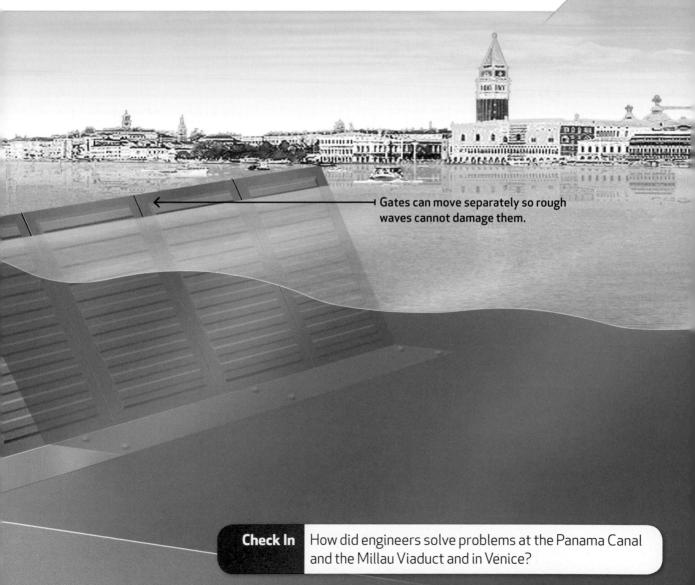

Gates can move separately so rough waves cannot damage them.

Check In How did engineers solve problems at the Panama Canal and the Millau Viaduct and in Venice?

Discuss

1. Tell about some of the ways you think the four pieces in this book are linked.

2. "Wonders of the World" describes ancient engineering feats. Name one problem builders were faced with in building each structure and how they solved it.

3. Compare the ways the structures in "How Tall!" solved the problem of wind damage.

4. What physical properties of the geography described in "Modern Engineering Feats" had to be overcome? Which seemed to you like they greatest challenge? Why?

5. What do you still wonder about how people actually live in tiny houses like those in "How Small!" Would you?